love is

Story and Pictures by Rachel K. Masterson

for dody, with love

Love is reading a book together.

Love is playing outside
in spite of the weather.

Love is a stroll through the park.

Love is a light
to brighten the dark.

Love is a song
whispered in your ear.

Love is missing

someone who isn't here.

Love is running

to greet you at the door.

Love is asking,
"just one more?"

Love is patient.

Love gives second chances.

Love SINGS, LAUGHS,

CRIES, and DANCES!

Love is a wink.

Love is a smile.

Love is

"stay for just a little while."

Love is a tummy to tickle
and a hand to hold.

Love warms you up
so you're never cold.

TOGETHER.

Made in the USA
San Bernardino, CA
09 December 2016